A Legend In Straw
The Spirit of My Uncle
Ray Bolger

A Legend In Straw
The Spirit of My Uncle
Ray Bolger

CHRISTIANNA RICKARD

YorkshirePublishing
www.yorkshirepublishing.com
Write Now.

ISBN: 978-1-947491-85-4
A Legend in Straw: The Spirit of my Uncle Ray Bolger
Copyright © 2010 by Christianna Rickard

Yorkshire Publishing
3207 South Norwood Avenue
Tulsa, Oklahoma 74135
www.YorkshirePublishing.com
918.394.2665

A Legend In Straw

is dedicated with great love to
my aunt and uncle, Gwen and
Ray Bolger; and to Uncle
Ray's well-loved counterpart,
the Scarecrow of Oz, who
touched our hearts and
showed us the way.

ACKNOWLEDGMENTS

I wish to thank talented artist, Vincent Myrand, for his fine cover portrait of Uncle Ray. Vincent cherished 'The Wizard of Oz' as a child and his artwork exemplifies the power and passion of the man. Vincent travels the country sharing his unique gifts as artist and teacher in a wide variety of venues. Influenced by his love of the Renaissance, Vincent's work transmits his deep commitment to fulfilling his life's purpose as an Ozian artist. Thank you so much, Vincent, for bringing Uncle Ray to life in such a poignant and potent way for the book.

The legendary Broadway photographer, Leo Friedman, kindly permitted me the use of his endearing pictures of my aunt and uncle. I thank him for his generous and open spirit to so graciously allow me to share them here. Hats off to a genius!

Finally, I must honor my dear friend, the writer, Jeanne M. Dallman. Her talent and life ended abruptly when lung cancer went too long undetected. Our literary friendship spanned four decades without a single boring moment. Jeanne, my exceptional friend, this book is for you, with the hope that future health care lets no one slip through the cracks as you did.

PREFACE

Several years after my uncle Ray died, I was strolling through a shopping mall when my eye caught something strangely familiar yet completely alien. It was my uncle, or rather, a life-sized scarecrow image of him swinging from the ceiling of a bookstore. He wasn't alone up there. Dorothy and Tin Man were there too. The Lion also dangled, quite precariously, I thought, from above. There were the four of them, all made of cardboard, suspended in space, connected to nothing, swaying lifelessly from the ceiling. But why?

I looked around the mall to see if anyone else recognized the madness of this scene. No one did. I sat down on a nearby bench to get a grip and sort it out. For in my view, Uncle Ray no more belonged up on that ceiling than I did, and I wanted to take him down, carry him to the car, and get him home as fast I could. The

Oz characters were my heroes, my friends, my family. They were immortals, worthy of the greatest respect and dignity. Black-and-white cardboard effigies hanging by a thread—unthinkable.

As unbelievable as it might seem today, that was my reaction that day in 1998. In that single moment, I realized that the world into which I had been birthed and woven had changed forever. The things that had held me together for the first forty years of my life would soon be replaced by images of the things I had known and loved. My memories of the flesh and blood Ray Bolger—his voice, his smell, his endlessly flowing arms and legs—would rapidly become less accessible to me, while his image would proliferate across the land and permeate the culture at lightning speed. In the future I saw I wouldn't be enjoying his company; I'd be buying it! Those swaying cardboard cutouts, innocuous enough to others, told me that something was strangely awry in Oz, and whatever it was, it was here to stay.

That's how it seemed to me. With several beloved family members passing away, one after another, taking their vivid personalities and memorable stories with them—their laughter, their music, their uncommon wisdom—I wondered what on earth would replace them. Would I learn to live in the new cardboard world? Could I survive on mere images?

I didn't have much time to ponder these questions, for a year later I was seriously ill. With my own dreams now dangling in limbo, I had to step out of the fabric of memory and nostalgia and onto the playing field of real life in the cancer ward. And what I realized when I hit the ground running was that I was a long, long way from home. With not a minute to waste, I forgave the bookstore for hanging the cardboard figures and set about to harness the energy and the imagination that the real Oz characters had given me while they were still alive.

As my journey through illness unfolded, I amassed some amazing insights and memories of my own. I made it my purpose to reassemble myself from the ground up and while at it to try to bring some fresh inspiration back to the kingdom. The kingdom of Oz, that is; that magical land we used to gather together to watch on TV one night a year. Before computers and cell phones and iPods. Before silence was silenced. We are only as well as the land we live in, and our land, I'm sure, is now in need of the same renewal and vitality I needed to get through cancer. This is a wake-up call. What is merely cardboard must go. What is alive must remain.

A Legend in Straw is, in part, a nostalgic look backward, but I hope it serves to help us remember our own land, to put its pieces back together and make it whole in the best way I know how, by telling a story. By taking time to look into our shared past and connect a few dots that may have scattered along the way, we can remember who we are and why we are here. In truth, the story is telling itself, and we are all a great and wonderful part of it.

So join me, travel with me. Bring your questions and your fears, your dangling dreams, your sorrows, your fire. Bring them all. There's nothing that's not sacred on this journey. We're off to see the Wizard, and there's no time to waste.

To Oz? To Oz!

A PESKY CROW

For six months, a small but clear voice in my head nagged at me like a bothersome black crow. "Call Betty! Call Betty!" it cawed over and over again. I didn't have the time or the patience to put up with its noisy nonsense. But one day, the crow said, "Call Betty now!" in a much more serious and louder than usual tone. I found the phonebook and dialed the one and only Betty I'd ever known.

Betty Wisener was a popular masseuse in the San Fernando Valley in Southern California. I'd seen her once or twice in recent years and remembered it could take weeks to get an appointment with her. But on this surprising day, she had a cancellation and would see me at two o'clock. What luck!

Betty did a wonderful job stretching muscles and working out every ache and pain in my tired but relatively fit body. Then, in the last five minutes of the luxurious massage, her deft, knowing fingers lingered a little too long and questioningly under my left collarbone. It seemed she'd stumbled onto something. "Something," she said, "that doesn't belong there."

Betty insisted I call my doctor as soon as I got home—the very minute. And the doctor too was eager to see me right away. I couldn't imagine what all the fuss could be about. The something, it turned out, was medullary thyroid carcinoma, a rare disease revealing itself in the form of a large, rock-hard lymph node buried beneath my collarbone. (Not a place I'd ever been told to look for unwanted lumps!) And with that, my house flew off its foundations, up into a whirling twister, and what felt like a one-way journey into strange, uncharted Oz-like territory began. It was cancer.

A year or so passes and two surgeries are performed. My thyroid and forty lymph nodes are removed, and some radiation is ingested. A twelve-inch scar wraps around my neck, squeezing uncomfortably like a tight turtleneck, but otherwise, I'm feeling fine. As good as new. Mind you, I'm not the same person I was. You can't really be the same once you've glimpsed your own death and you know for certain that life is a brief, temporary journey. Any illusions I had of being indestructible in any but the most cosmic sense are well behind me. I'm in a whole different world now. My old outlook doesn't seem to work here, and the new one hasn't really appeared.

I'm just like Dorothy, heading for the gates of the Emerald City, where old dreams can be shined up like new and where the unexpected happens at every turn. The Emerald City, home of the great and powerful Wizard of Oz. "Where's the Wizard?" I ask. "Will he grant my wish or help me get back to that illusory place I once thought of as home?"

To understand what this imagery means to me, I'm going deep down inside myself to resurrect the big, magical Oz of my childhood. I'll try to retrace my steps and gather the bits and pieces of the puzzle that somehow became my own story—just as *The Wonderful Wizard of Oz* was the great myth and story of my uncle Ray, the dancing Scarecrow. And just as your life is its own story, unfolding in and dancing through you right now.

This isn't a biography of my uncle but my living

memory of him and the things he taught me. Vivid things I can never forget. It's a journey through my mind, a place full of chattering munchkins, intoxicating flower fields, and some very frightening monkeys with big, flapping wings. A place like your mind, full of beauty and terror, hopes, dreams, and fantasies.

It's a journey I wouldn't have had the courage to make until I got cancer. But now, in order to stay well and alive, I have to make the journey. I have to follow the one true Yellow Brick Road that my uncle promised me leads to home. The forest ahead looks a little dark and creepy, and I suspect it may not be an easy trip. But, like Dorothy and the dear old Scarecrow, we can make it through together, hand in hand. With love and courage, and faith in our vision, we can survive and prevail.

There are connections between the journey through cancer and the journey through Oz. There are stories to be told and life lessons learned. Uncle Ray never taught me to put stock in the world, not in institutions or authority figures, and certainly not in technology. He was a dancer, a storyteller, and an artist. He put stock in his body, in his two feet and his creative spirit. He put stock in love and family and his own strong sense of purpose. His inspiration and vision were strongly encouraged by his wife, Gwen, and strengthened by his faith in the living Lord of his own dance.

Unable to have children of their own, my aunt and uncle's desire to influence the next generation landed on my brothers, my cousins, and me. The things my uncle said and the way he leaped through our lives were deeply imprinted on my young psyche. And years later, when I found myself with cancer and scared half to death, those unforgettable psychic imprints played a huge role in my life's journey. Could my memories of my uncle and the magical world of Oz hold a key to my survival?

MEET THE
SCARECROW

The Wizard of Oz is one of the most familiar stories—if not the most familiar story—of our generation. Its countless images are imprinted on *all* of our psyches in ways we can scarcely imagine. More references are made to Oz every single day, in every form of media in our land, than to any other book or movie in history. But though the story lives in us at deep, subconscious levels, we often fail to remember its wisdom and use it in our daily lives. Why not wake these slumbering memories up and let them jump back into life feet first? We may find ourselves responding to just about everything with greater clarity, renewed vitality, and a quicker step.

I seldom meet a person these days who doesn't perk up at the mention of my uncle Ray's name. Why do they respond so eagerly, I often wonder? I think it's because *The Wizard of Oz* is our shared journey story, and we know the Scarecrow as a deeply loyal guide and friend. Every year we followed him down the Yellow Brick Road, counting on his common sense to pull out life-saving answers at the eleventh hour. We trusted him to do his utmost for Dorothy and Toto, and he always did. And he did it all without a brain! What was his secret? Where did his clarity, his common sense, and his sharp instincts come from?

The Scarecrow of my family worked hard to keep us awake to the presence of a richer, more colorful and wonder-filled world, a world we must pay attention to now. For the Scarecrow is a guardian who holds vigil over our deepest dreams and all that our hearts and minds hold dear. His humble image dots our landscape everywhere you look these days, catching our intuitive eye, reminding us to be watchful and awake, to listen, and to stay on the right path with ourselves and others. His eyes are wide open, his heart is true, and his wisdom and practical guidance have never been needed more.

Just like the Scarecrow, Uncle Ray knew the path he wanted us to follow, and he was nothing if not an enthusiastic and uninhibited guide. Every year at Christmas dinner, he gathered our large family together in a circle, leading us in his own unique Oz-style prayer. After painting a moving portrait of Jesus nestled safely in the warm straw of the manger, he paid eloquent tribute to the family members no longer with us, honoring and including them in our family circle. Then, when stillness and awe settled in over us in their soft, mysterious way, he started his chant for love. First, he clapped his hands and set a rhythmic beat, drumming up energy in the circle like a tribal shaman. Then he jumped up and down, clapping his hands. We were instructed to hold hands and jump up and down with him, calling out in our loudest voices, "Love! Love! Love!"

"Louder," he cried. "Shout it out! It's all about love!" he sang, like a kid starting a love club, a funny flower child in full bloom. We all thought he was completely over the top, but as patriarch of the family, if he said that was the way to pray, he probably knew best. So we jumped and we shouted, and that was that.

And now, many years later, I know that he was right. Love is worth jumping up and down about and even raising the roof with a little shouting. His fine demonstration of totally free, unorthodox spirituality got my attention at a very early age and led me down a path of exploration and learning I may never have otherwise taken.

As much as he enjoyed his celebrity status and all that went with it—performing throughout the world, dining with heads of state, teaching in foreign lands, enjoying fans, and exemplifying *the good life* in every imaginable sense—Uncle Ray was never more than a second away from slipping into a deep, focused state of mind, especially when it came to Oz. In his childhood, his much loved mother tucked him into bed at night and read all of L. Frank Baum's great adventure books aloud to him. The stories shaped his first impressions of life and kept him awake into the wee hours, his vivid imagination dancing with incredible images and ideas. Could such remarkable things really exist?

When his mother died suddenly and much too young, her gentle voice, intertwined with the magical words of those stories, kept her memory alive in my uncle Ray forever. Growing up to actually become the Scarecrow from the books made the laws and lessons of Oz practically indisputable truth! Uncle Ray quoted the story to us continuously, slipping in and out of characters, outrageous voices, and screeching witches' cackles to put his point across. He was having great fun, but then, with sudden urgency, he told us to hear the profound wisdom of the story.

The Wizard of Oz, he would say, transports us to a different dimension of life. A mysterious but very real dimension where the secrets of life are shared and the things that really matter are revealed. *Courage, brains, heart, and home!* These are the things to remember, he insisted. And believe me, when you're a child of six, seven, and eight and the Scarecrow of Oz, himself, tells you something's magical and important and must be remembered…you listen! Certainly, I did.

My uncle showed us how to use space, energy and movement, leaping through the living room like an Irish leprechaun one minute, spinning and gliding around like a graceful gazelle the next. Almost always in motion, his limber body and his expressive face were the tools of his trade. He spoke of the need to grow and expand, to work with inspiration and freedom, and to give generously from the flowing springs of our imaginations.

Something he impressed upon me many times throughout the years, in a way I never forgot, was that I needed to be with people. "Be with the people," he would say, waving a finger my way. "You must be with the people." As a child, and for many years to follow, I wasn't at all sure what he meant. Now I think I know.

Never think you're less or greater than any other person. You're unique in the family of humankind, but you're not separate from anyone. Despite what we may imagine, what defenses we hold up, or what masks we may wear, we're all family, and love itself turns the circle of life that holds us all together. Don't be a missing link. Find your rhythm and play your part with and among others. That's what I took from his admonition. Make friends with all humanity and know yourself as one important part of a whole and interdependent world.

This was an important lesson for me as a child, for more often than not I stood to the side of things, detached and observing. "You must be with the people," I can still hear my uncle saying, and I'm glad he persisted with the message. My cancer journey prompted a great need to rediscover who I was, where I had come from, and where I might be going. And with that deep urge came a much deeper desire to connect in love with all those traveling the precarious road through life with me. Often we have to look back on a situation after many years to truly understand its full significance. Those few puzzling words, *be with the people,* stayed with me as if they'd come straight from the mouth of the Wizard of Oz himself.

When sudden disaster or misfortune strikes, the shock of change throws us miles out of our normal orbits and far out of our comfort zones. The illusion of our separateness vanishes quickly, and we turn to one another as brothers and sisters united by a common goal. Seeing our wholeness shattered to pieces, we suddenly remember its inestimable value. We drop the amnesia and paralysis of the previous moment and hurry to shore up members of the family most in need. We pull on strength we'd forgotten we had and behave like mighty angels on a mission from God.

These times of crisis, while frightening, reveal our innate strength and integrity, which ultimately surpass and outshine our vulnerability. They inspire and empower the best in us, and we all agree it's wonderful to see and to feel—at least for a time. But how do we sustain this remarkable spirit of unity when the crisis passes?

The Scarecrow might answer this way: Focus on the living spirit of love that animates all life and moves through and among all of us. Recognize it as an important and precious gift... as *the* important and precious gift of life. We're not separate. We're one. And we're happiest when, in unity with our neighbors, we become much greater than the sum of our parts. We'll rise to our highest level of achievement and happiness when we join together and work for the good of all. We are all mysteriously connected to one another, and on some level, *we know it*. Remembering this takes us a long way down the road toward home.

There are many theories and perspectives about cancer, but little is really known other than that the disease is rampant and difficult to contain. I believe the greatest disease of our day is the separation of parts from the whole, which is what cancer cells are all about. Going off on their own, these misfit cells don't identify with the bigger game plan of keeping the body alive and whole. They have their own mis-informed agenda, and they plan to get away with it. How do we rein them in?

A diagnosis of cancer calls us to search our hearts, reset our priorities, and reflect on the need for extremely wise transformation. Our world is changing very quickly now, and it seems to be moving toward fragmentation and disintegration rather than in the direction of unity and love. "Love, love, love," my spir-ited uncle chanted. It's a word we know so well and agree is a good and necessary thing. But how do we embody it and share it so that love sweeps across the country faster than the rapidly growing rate of cancer?

My uncle Ray had cancer. Ironically, it went to his brain. And Aunt Gwen, his elegant wife, had both of her breasts removed because of breast cancer. We all carry some cancer cells in our bodies, and the risk of imbalance is always there—in our bodies and in our world. But both my aunt and my uncle lived long, fulfilling lives, and I believe I know why. The things I learned from them may help us live better, more balanced lives. Lives that connect our courage, brains, and hearts and help us see life as an opportunity to strengthen ourselves as we support one another. Then, one fine day, we may make our world a truly suitable home for the love we are here to express.

My journey into unknown territory began the day I got shattering news of a life-threatening illness. But we're all on a strange, disorienting journey these days, it seems. The sense of security we grew up with toppled before our disbelieving eyes one early September morning. The dust eventually settled, but clarity never really returned. Jolting experiences like these bring us instantly to entirely new places in our lives. Scary, confusing places that we have to face with courage, intelligence, and most of all, with tremendous love for ourselves and all of life. We need to remember the very important meaning of our story, find our place in it, and build on a true foundation laid by those who've journeyed well and bravely before us. *We need to remember who we are.*

Just as the entire landscape of Oz thrilled early

viewers by shifting in an instant from black and white to bright, blooming Technicolor, so our world is shifting to a new and amazing kind of world. Many undreamed of possibilities and perspectives are opening up before our eyes. The clear-cut, black-and-white approach to life is collapsing in front of our faces, and we may feel frightened and uncertain. But *we* are not collapsing. And for those with eyes and hearts and minds to imagine it, a rainbow can still be seen on the distant horizon.

OUR CHILDHOOD STORY

MGM's *The Wizard of Oz* opened in 1939 with the following line: "For forty years, this story has given faithful service to the young at heart, and time has been powerless to put its kindly philosophy out of fashion." Now, over a hundred years have passed, and the story still inspires the best in us and remains in fashion for the youngest of us. Adventure, friendship and family, and the purpose of the hero's journey to find home are the themes that continue to shape our American souls.

A great story like *The Wizard of Oz* has a life of its own, a life that never dies. It passes through us, becomes part of who we are, and continues on far beyond us. It binds us together in hope and fear as we watch it, jogging memories of our own troubles and our own wisdom, inspiring us to find new ways to face our own shifting, shaking world. The heroes of Oz model courage, creativity, and cooperation, and they show us how our most severe challenges can make us stronger, more humane human beings.

I'm writing these memories as if writing down snippets from an amazing dream. Not everything fits together neatly nor makes perfect sense to me. Life is a collection of experiences we seldom have time to sort out and piece together into an elegant, seamless whole. Events stack up and time flies, psyches rearrange themselves, and the story charges on, changing directions every minute. Yet, in taking the time to write the images and memories down, connections are made, forms take shape, and I begin to see my part in this mysterious Oz-like journey. Your part too may lie hidden within these pages. It may be a call to a specific task, or it may lead you to a deeper, clearer understanding of your life's true value or purpose. You hold a unique place in this fast-changing landscape of life. The journey was well designed and is even now unfolding according to a wiser plan than you can ever imagine.

Perhaps something in you is getting ready to

speak or to act, nudging you in the direction you have most wanted to go. The Yellow Brick Road lies before you. It leads to the dazzling Emerald City of your deepest dream. What will you ask the Wizard for when you arrive? What is it that your heart really desires? Are you ready to follow?

For my uncle Ray, the philosophy of Oz was the center of his life. He listened to its wisdom and danced down his own Yellow Brick Road all of his days. Though he left this world some time ago, he still inspires me to return to the Yellow Brick Road when I stray from it, for it is a good path, a true and reliable one. It's a path which can ground us for both the wonderful and the perilous adventures we know lie ahead.

There's no manual for this journey to Oz, no Web site, no expert to consult. And you certainly can't get there by a boat or a train. This is a slow motion journey to the quiet center of the cyclone of your own being, where every moment is alive with possibility. When you listen to and gather enough of these moments together, strength begins to build in you, and the scattered pieces of your life begin to form a pattern of rare and beautiful wholeness.

Like many great stories throughout time, *The Wizard of Oz* takes us on a journey to a larger awareness of who we are, why we're here, and what we are capable of. To navigate the journey, we turn to the subtle world of listening and guidance. We grow in wisdom as we go, becoming less fearful and surer of ourselves. Soon we are kinder and more sensitive to ourselves and to others. Old knee-jerk reactions give way to more insightful choices. Pleasant thoughts become potent realities. Life reveals itself as a living story, in which we each play a strong and vital role. And like the Scarecrow watching over the vast fields of time, we can see for miles and miles.

Jesus called this abundant viewpoint the kingdom of heaven, saying that light is in each of us, shining on our path. In *The Wizard of Oz,* Dorothy calls it a land over the rainbow where dreams come true. Great teachers use story and symbols to speak their wisdom into our keen, knowing souls. They invite us to listen with open hearts and to see our overly conditioned lives with new eyes. They awaken us and help us look beyond the judgments and fears that blind us. Soon we begin to see our questions tied to solutions as near to us as our next breath. The Emerald City is here, all around us. It's in us!

The Wizard of Oz is an encyclopedia of these images and symbols. Poppies point to our habit of falling asleep at the wrong moments, twisters show sudden change or destruction, and the rainbow captures our capacity to look for the miraculous on any horizon. Symbols speak a universal language of our deepest feelings and dreams, showing us life's greatest, but often veiled, possibilities.

My uncle Ray embodied this symbolic world every day of his life, and much of it he passed on to me. When my life took a big turn for the worse, I began to realize the gifts I had received from him. *When had the poppies put me to sleep?* I asked myself. *What caused the cyclone in my life? Would a rainbow ever be possible for me now?*

JUST BE YOU!

"Always be yourself!" Uncle Ray used to tell me. "Why try to be something you're not? Be you!" He learned early on in his career that not trusting his own instincts and style of expression brought disastrous results. He and a fellow comedian, Ralph Sanford, were coaxed by a popular showman of their day into dressing their comedy routine up with dashing derby hats and spats and presenting themselves as a sophisticated team called Bolger and Sanford: A Pair of Nifties.

After the opening night show, the theater manager rapped on their dressing room door, glared in, and muttered, "Nifties, huh?" The next day, they arrived at work to find a note tacked on the locked theater door. "*Nifties: Canceled!*" said it all. From that moment on, my uncle said, he forgot about trying to be nifty, suave, or dapper and decided to concentrate on being who he really was—original and funny, with a powerful urge to create his own unique and eccentric dance form. "Be yourself," he said adamantly. "That's the thing!"

What could be easier than that, you ask? Just being yourself? But is it really so easy, or is it, in reality, one of life's greatest challenges and most important goals? A gripping scene from *The Wizard of Oz,* which often brought me to tears as a little girl, brings this issue of our identity into clear focus. When at last they're granted entrance to see the great and powerful Oz, Dorothy and her friends, all newly coifed and cleaned, are reduced to quivering jelly as they stand before the roaring, fiery, disembodied head. In this poignant portrayal of human vulnerability, we watch in agony as each of the four steps forward to reply to the Wizard's booming demand to know, "*Whoooo are youuu?*" Clearly, he's not looking for unimpressive answers.

Dorothy takes the first timid step down the huge echoing corridor and identifies herself. "I'm Dorothy...the small and meek." One by one the others follow, cowering and falling to the floor as the would-be Wizard terrifies and demeans him. But when at last she's seen enough of his abuse, Dorothy breaks the spell of her smallness and meekness and demands an explanation for the Wizard's outlandish, tyrannical behavior. When it came to defending someone weaker than herself, Dorothy had no trouble remembering who she was. Something far stronger possessed her and acted boldly and instinctively through her. In that moment, Dorothy was being herself. Unhindered by social conditioning or restraints, she simply responded naturally and directly.

Growing up with the Bolgers often prompted me to think about the bigger issues of my life. It could be daunting at times to relay my various career schemes and misadventures to my uncle's wife. Much like the Wizard, my powerful and discerning Aunt Gwen didn't go in for a whole lot of fluff. In response to my many stories, she'd often look up over the top of her reading glasses, raise her eyebrows, and ask me in a curious, sober tone, "Did you tell them who you are?"

I was always puzzled by the question, not sure what it meant or how to answer it. While I assumed she wondered if I made a practice of mentioning Uncle Ray's name to people (I didn't), the question seemed to carry a deeper, more cryptic meaning. Aunt Gwen seldom said *anything* that was without some deeper insight or purpose. *Tell them who I am?* The question rattled around my mind like a riddle designed to unravel me. Does anyone want to know who I am? Who I *really* am? For that matter, do I really know?

My aunt and I always ended our visits on a more provocative note than they had begun, and I left the house feeling far more challenged and intrigued about life than when I had arrived. Tell them who I am. Now that was a real head scratcher!

Something at the heart of a crisis like cancer demands an answer to this perplexing question. With sand slipping too quickly through the hourglass, a counterforce of accelerated will to find and be one's authentic self arises quickly. Masks of inadequacy, timidity, and equivocation must be stripped off, and one must stand up for oneself in a clear and powerful way. No stumbling. No apologizing. Just stepping forward with courage, calling forth that which belongs to each of us simply by virtue of being born human into an often less than humane world. What is called forth is our universal, God-given right to dignity and self-respect. It's our native instinct for protecting life and caring for ourselves and those we love. And as we see with Dorothy and her companions, these powerful callings are often brought to the fore in the supportive and sometimes challenging company of our closest allies. *We do know who we are.* We just need to be reminded.

A crisis is a good reminder, a wake-up call. But remembering all the time... that's the challenge. Fortunately, every bit of know-how we need to help us be our authentic selves has come down to us on the lips of storytellers and wisdom keepers throughout the ages. We are not alone in our challenge. We never have been, never will be. The wisdom is here. The kingdom is now. We just need to wake up, remember it, and bring it forward into life. It's always ours to choose. And that's good news.

My answer to the "who am I" question has changed since I had cancer. My friends and companions don't always see or understand the shifts in perception that have occurred in me, and I can't easily explain what I mean when I tell them certain things in life just don't matter as they used to.

Now, knowing I am far more than a limited, fearful creature whose value must continually be proven is what matters. Instead of struggling with all the details of life myself, I put a lot of them into God's hands. I listen more carefully to the life around me. I try to notice the subtler things. I help when I feel that my help is needed. And I remain silent when more voices don't seem called for. It's a continuous learning process that is always new and fascinating and always full of surprises.

Not long ago, a good friend pointed out that in the course of our brief conversation, I used the terms "on the hook" and "hung up" repeatedly. I had pointed to the scar surrounding my neck and said that it looked like a big fish hook.

"Listen to you," she said earnestly. "Do you hear what you're saying?"

"No. What did I say?" I replied innocently.

"Hang ups, on the hook, hooks around your neck... You've got yourself hung up on a hook!"

Startled, I realized she was right. At that particular moment, I was hooked on hang-ups, and I hadn't heard a single word I'd said. The hooks and hang-ups are the countless expectations and demands we place on ourselves (and others) too much of the time, often without even realizing we're doing it! I let out a deep sigh of recognition. My shoulders dropped about a foot, and I felt my breath start to flow freely through my body once again.

Suddenly, I remembered Uncle Ray hanging up on a pole by the side of the Yellow Brick Road in Oz. He was calling out to Dorothy to turn down the nail that had kept him up on a hook for ages, waiting for a kind soul to come along and set him free. My own kind and attentive friend had seen that I too needed a help-ing hand to slide off the pole and be free of tyrannical thoughts that were hanging me up. It was a wonderful relief to move and breathe freely again, and I set off with a new insight into the workings of my mind.

Now I can ask myself at any given moment, "Am I freely and fully being myself at this moment? Am I breathing freely or holding my breath? Is my body feeling relaxed, or is it rigid? Am I being truthful and real? If not, what's the hang-up? What can I do right now to get free, to wake up and come back to life?" That's *Life* with a capital L when I'm awake and aware of the present moment and the potential that it holds.

"Be yourself," my uncle told me, and how right he was. There's no more need to exaggerate our significance in life than there is to try to minimize it. Just be you. Accept yourself as you are, right where you are now. Express yourself honestly, simply. Be present, in the present. Not just one or two parts of you, but all of you. And when you're awake and moving in harmony with the present moment, the great positive forces of the universe can help you and use you to help others.

Dorothy's name may have some significance in *The Wizard of Oz*. It comes from the Greek root words *Doron* and *Thea*, which mean *gift of* and *God*. Dorothy might represent each one of us as a unique gift and expression of God, a human being on a journey of discovery. Oh, hooks and hang-ups snare us at times, and we learn a great deal from them. But life is a continuously flowing gift to and through us, and Dorothy represents the spark of our remembering, our desire to wake up and be more loving, more courageous, and more responsive to the life that's in and all around us.

When we face illness or loss in our lives, knowing that our journey through life is a spiritual journey can be a haven of sanity and peace. There is much more to life than meets the eye, and we are never really alone. At those wonderful times when we remember this, we can be beacons of hope to those who have yet to find their way home. This is no time to shrink from sight, to hold back, or wonder about your value. Being fully you, in whatever condition you find yourself today, is what matters most of all. Let your light shine in you and through you to others. Whether it's glowing very softly or burning brightly on this particular day, it's the gift you are given and the gift you are here to give. Throw the rule book out, take a nice deep breath, and let yourself just be you.

THE YELLOW
BRICK ROAD

Raymond Wallace Bolger set off down his Yellow
Brick Road as a lanky, limber youth with a strong
desire to express himself and have fun, and his destiny seemed to unfold naturally from his buoyant
spirit. After a dismal display of ineptitude at a high
school dance in his hometown of Dorchester, Mas-
sachusetts, he set off to learn some basic waltz steps
well enough to redeem himself with the girls. Shortly
into his efforts, he was spotted by Boston's ballet
master, Senia Rusikov. In exchange for free book-
keeping services, Rusikov took Uncle Ray's raw talent and energetic spirit and gave them the discipline
and shape they needed to find their real meaning.

Always hardworking and enthusiastic, my uncle
had an energy level that never quite jibed with that
of the New England Insurance Company or the First

National Bank, where he soon began to work. On more than one occasion, the sound of his tapping feet aroused the ire of his superiors. Though he enjoyed the work well enough, his feet wouldn't cooperate. Then, one day in 1921, at a coworker's insistence, he did something he had never done before. He went to the theater. He bought an upper balcony ticket for twenty-five cents and went to see a fellow named Fred Stone dancing up a storm in a show called *Jack O'Lantern*. And that was all he needed. "A world of enchantment opened up before my eyes," my uncle later said, "a world I knew I had to belong to."

Fred Stone's enchanted world reflected more about Uncle Ray's life and future than he could have imagined. For in 1904, the year my uncle was born, the first production of *The Wizard of Oz* opened on Broadway, with Fred Stone playing ... the Scarecrow! Years later, these two kindred song-and-dance men met and formed their own mutual admiration society ... fellow straw men on the Yellow Brick Road of life.

Bob Ott's musical-comedy repertoire company and numerous Vaudeville adventures consumed the next few years, as my uncle traveled the country working his gifts as comedic dancer, singer, and actor into a versatile, entertaining package. Things were starting to come together. But it wasn't until his outgoing and physical nature met up with the sharp eye and keen instincts of my aunt Gwen that his gifts began to blend into a wholeness that eventually brought him Broadway stardom. In spite of his long Tony Award-winning career on the stage, however, Uncle Ray always knew that his greatest legacy with the public would be his memorable film portrayal of Scarecrow, Dorothy's dearest ally on the Yellow Brick Road through Oz.

Along my journey through cancer, I felt much like Dorothy. From the outset of the journey, she and I had one goal—to get back to where we had started from without further ado. But as we all know, it's neither quite that fast nor quite that easy to do. First, I had a long, winding road to travel, allies to meet, and setbacks, difficulties, and discouragements to overcome.

With no knowledge of where I was headed, I had to figure out who and what my allies were and who they were not. I met all types of people, some helpful and understanding beyond my wildest dreams, and others with little insight into the mind of a person newly diagnosed with cancer. It was important for me to rely on my own instincts, to discern whom I wanted to share my journey with. *If things get worse,* I'd ask myself, *is this someone I'd want to spend my last days with?* In a last-days frame of mind, I assure you, honest, heartfelt communication quickly becomes the only kind worth engaging in.

What it is that made Dorothy's companions such wonderful allies on the Yellow Brick Road? It seems to me that three things were involved. First, they faced and accepted the realities of their present situations. Second, they chose to seek a better way of life. And third, they were willing to face the risks that all change requires.

They acknowledged where they were. They longed for something more. They chose to take the risk. Who of us these days easily admits, "I have no clue what I'm doing with my life. I can't figure it out or get anything right?" Or, "Life has beaten me down. I'm weary, and I no longer hear the early song of my heart." Or, "I have great dreams and ambitions, but I lack the courage to execute them." These were the predicaments of the three hapless travelers who joined Dorothy on the Yellow Brick Road.

I needed doctors who weren't threatened by my vulnerability, or by their own, who weren't more afraid I might not reach the Emerald City alive than I was. I conveyed my feelings to them, though my words often filled their scientific spaces with all the congruence of a monkey in the sky. I made my position clear and did what I could to elicit the deeper awareness of the medical staff. I wanted to reach them in any way I could, often saying plainly, "I'm really scared," or asking, "Do you believe in God?" By revealing my inner thoughts, I took a risk. I would appear foolish and out of place, or they would go deeper with me and the journey would be a shared one. The flatter my commentary fell, the more quickly I moved on down the road.

Any adventure that will yield growth holds risk and the potential for loss. I love Dorothy's insight when she says to the Scarecrow, "Well, even if he doesn't [give you a brain], you'll be no worse off than you are now!" Often we're so afraid of losing what we have, what we cling so tightly to, that we don't accept opportunities for what is new in life. But we have nothing truly vital when we block the arrival of the spontaneous and the unexpected.

The story of Oz is one of continuous surprise, continuous encounter with the unknown, and that's why we love it. There is a thrill, a feeling of aliveness, when we embark on a journey from which we may or may not ever return. And we're all on that journey from birth until death—whether we realize it or not.

One day in 1926, a teenage girl not much older than Dorothy arrived at the Orpheum Theater in Los Angeles, hoping to peddle her newly written songs. The girl had traveled a good distance from her prairie roots in Montana and carried within her the seeds of a large destiny. The eldest child of four, the only daughter, little Gwendolyn Rickard stalwartly took charge of raising her three younger brothers as her mother's refined mind and spiritual outlook were poorly suited to life in cold, harsh conditions. Aunt Gwen never had a bedroom of her own and slept on a couch in the small living room until she was twelve years old.

She did, however, have a mirror of her own, and in it, she saw the reflection of a very different life to come. I will never forget her telling me of the day she looked into that mirror and told herself, with undiluted resolve, "*You* are going to *be* someone!" Her vivid recollection of that single moment of decision was undiminished. Poplar, Montana, it seems, would never be big enough to hold the dreams of this precocious, visionary young girl. Her Yellow Brick Road was beckoning, "Follow!" and she was eager to heed the call.

A strong, natural inclination to lead and to see possibilities made my aunt a dominant figure in the household as the years brought hardship and crises to the family. When the baby of the family was shot in the eye by a neighborhood ruffian, my grandfather packed the family up and moved to a Spanish-style bungalow on Martel Avenue in sunny West Hollywood, California.

Eventually that brother, sporting what I always assumed was a pirate's patch, became a highly-respected surgeon, his eye patch stitched strong with love and his education paid for entirely by his loyal, protective older sister, Gwen.

After graduating far ahead of schedule from Fairfax High School, my aunt pursued a career as a journalist, selling her musical compositions where she could along the way. But little did she know that her looking-glass prophecy was about to come true the day she set foot into Gus Edward's Orpheum Theater. She always insisted, however, that the second she laid eyes on Uncle Ray, the funny-looking beanpole in the baggy pants up on the Orpheum's stage, she told herself, "There's the man I am going to marry." And two years later, marry him she did.

The Bolger creative partnership fell quickly into place, and within a few years, the pair were on their way. With Aunt Gwen reading scripts, negotiating contracts, and managing everything from furnishings to finances (her good taste landed Uncle Ray on 1949's list of best-dressed American men), my uncle was free to perfect the dance wizardry that soon saw them easing their way down the road to Broadway.

The critics stood up and took notice when Uncle Ray emerged in a show called *By Jupiter* as not only a dancer but a satirist of great subtlety. Solid hit shows like *Three to Make Ready* and *Life Begins at 8:40* kept

the young couple living in high style at the Waldorf
Towers on Park Avenue for years to come. *On Your
Toes,* in which Uncle Ray danced the George Bal-
anchine ballet, "Slaughter on Tenth Avenue," led to
many lucrative opportunities.

By 1947, my aunt was coproducing *Where's Charley?,* a long-running musical sensation directed by
George Abbott and choreographed, again, by Bal-
anchine. Uncle Ray starred in a demanding dual role
as college student Charlie Wykeham and Charlie's
wildly-eccentric aunt, Donna Lucia, from Brazil.
By this time, Aunt Gwen had earned a reputation
around New York as a savvy, no-nonsense business-
woman. The first female producer of a hit Broadway show, she knew what she wanted and how to get
it. When a tall, blonde Texas girl named Katharine
Reeve auditioned for the chorus during her first trip
to New York City, my aunt took one look at her and
said, "I want her!" She got her, and the fate of the
young Texas songbird was sealed.

One day, during a busy rehearsal at the St. James
Theater, Gwen's brother Jim stopped by to see how
things were going. Jim Rickard, who was then writ-

ing screenplays and running a business with young Robert Altman, spotted the new singer onstage and smiled at her. Later that week he took her to the 21 Club for dinner with my aunt and uncle, and within a year, my parents, James and Katharine, were married on a hilltop under a big, starry West Texas sky.

When I listen to *Where's Charley?*'s exuberant hit song "Once in Love with Amy," I feel the excitement audiences must have felt singing the song aloud with Uncle Ray during the show. "Amy" became his signature song, and when I listen to it I wonder if I once watched this family collaboration from somewhere beyond the stars, waiting to make my entrance onto the stage of life. However things may actually work, these were the characters I would one day follow down my own Yellow Brick Road.

We each have a unique Yellow Brick Road to follow. This life path or blueprint is often discouraged by our cultural systems or by our families and must be reestablished by means of a difficult series of events, such as the journey through Oz. Where would Dorothy and her friends be without the Yellow Brick Road to keep them on course? Winding deeper and deeper into the dark woods, I'm afraid. It's their commitment to following the Yellow Brick Road to the end that keeps them going in the right direction.

What can we say about yellow brick roads? Well, they aren't poured in overnight like slabs of concrete. They're laid in carefully, brick by brick. Each brick is fitted next to the other with precision and care, one brick at a time. The color yellow suggests the brightness of an awakened mind with its silent knowledge, original ideas, and rich insights. It's a hopeful, radiant color we associate with the strong life force of the sun and the dawning of a new day. And the road itself is the solid, reliable earth beneath our feet. We trust it to be there each time we take our next step forward. I like to imagine the Yellow Brick Road as a path that combines our disciplined efforts in the external world with our deep inner guidance and intuitive direction. It's a road that respects all aspects of who we are, blending the dense clay of our physical selves with the dreams of our hearts and the visions of our higher minds.

What direction are you going in? What do you want to accomplish while here on earth? Is now the time to begin? Do you have a vision, a sense of direction, and a firm, reliable road beneath your feet? Your Yellow Brick Road will sustain you when you may feel you have lost your way. You can return to it, knowing it is solid and sure beneath your feet. It may be your dream of fulfilling a talent you have. It may be a spiritual practice or a physical discipline you follow, values or works to which you are dedicated. It is a path you will never forget ... and if you do forget, it will not forget you. It's your journey, your road, and in times of sudden transition or turmoil, you'll never regret that at least a few of your yellow bricks were in a row.

Uncle Ray entertained the troops in the Pacific with the USO.

A dapper young Ray Bolger.

Aunt Gwen - a chic and savvy force to be reckoned with!

Aunt Gwen handling the family finances.

*He was a show-stopping dancer, but Uncle Ray
considered himself a comedian first. "Muscles
with a sense of humor," said one critic.*

*Virtually everything my aunt and uncle
did was a creative collaboration.*

The Bolgers celebrating with Grandfather Rickard in his homeland of Hawaii.

*Uncle Ray's performance as the clever, lovable
Scarecrow of Oz captured our imaginations forever.*

Dorothy meets her first ally on the Yellow Brick Road.
Uncle Ray always spoke of Judy with the greatest affection.

Uncle Ray playing matchmaker for my mom and dad. He introduced them in his dressing room during the run of "Where's Charley?"

A moment of concentration before bursting onto the scene in
"Where's Charley?" at the St. James Theater.

*Uncle Ray in full drag as Charley's aunt. My mom, then Katharine
Reeve, is looking down from his upper right. She said she learned
something new every single time she watched Uncle Ray perform.*

After 50 years of marriage Uncle Ray said of Aunt Gwen,
"She's still the most interesting person I know."
"This is a love affair that will never end," said Aunt Gwen.

Uncle Ray as limber at seventy years old as when
he played the Scarecrow. One newspaper wrote,
"Bolger claims he is 68, looks 38, and moves like he's 28!"

YOU'RE SURE TO GET A BRAIN

"If I only had a brain," the Scarecrow sang, a tune as melodic and uplifting today as it was decades ago. Some of those wonderful lyrics by Yip Harburg and Harold Arlen were written on the old, ornately painted grand piano that sits in my mother's living room today. I still love to play the songs from *The Wizard of Oz* from time to time, so touching and clever. "Well, what would you do with a brain if you had one?" Dorothy asks the Scarecrow.

Not a bad question at all. Scarecrow replies that if he had a brain, he'd confer with flowers and consult with the rain. He'd unravel riddles for "individels" in trouble and pain. Good choices, I think. Uncle Ray delighted himself in the simple details of life. As a boy of humble origins, he learned early to find magic in the small things. He was sixteen when his mother died and his father left town for good. My uncle became adept at creating family and friends wherever he happened to find himself, and this talent never left him.

Inevitably, if I took a friend or two to his house for a swim, he would run upstairs and don his trunks, come out, and jump in the pool with us, carrying on like a goofy older brother and having a ball. He always pointed out something of beauty in the yard, my aunt's colorful roses or the enormous rubber tree overhead, demanding that we share in his vision, in his passion for life. He was truly, almost ecstatically, in tune with the life of the moment and his surroundings.

He taught me to look at things more closely, to see them more deeply. See them, smell them, touch them, think about them, and appreciate them. Not to settle for skimming the surface of life but to look until I could sense and feel the essence of things and know them in new and vital ways.

This is good medicine for our age, I believe. Slowing down and seeing the beauty in what surrounds us. Realizing that we are a wonderful, unique part of a whole, living world. A natural world of great beauty, power, and oneness that supports all of us every minute of the day. A world whose survival now depends largely on our wisdom and good judgment.

It seems to me we've strayed too far from using our brains to communicate with the natural world and to see the real solutions to the sufferings of humanity and the harming of the planet. When diagnosed with cancer, I became very frightened, a reasonable reaction. But my fear of the disease and where it would lead me was quickly superseded by a deeper fear of the treatment. I would soon be immersed in the business of medicine, a business I thought might be devoid of all natural wisdom or intuitive insight, a business I wanted no part of.

I realized I'd have to use my own brain to learn about my rare form of thyroid cancer. I would research it, understand it, and enter the hectic, high-tech medical world ready to represent myself and have my say in every decision. I followed my profoundest instincts to select doctors who understood my need to be in charge of my own life, to be true to myself, and to talk openly about what I was experiencing.

Doctors such as these do exist, but I had to abandon a few along the way whose attitudes were more frightening than reassuring to me. There were many questions to ask, things to learn, and tough decisions to make. I raced around the Internet and gathered information from relatives and friends of friends who knew other friends. I talked to doctors in other states, swinging from hope to despair on a minute-by-minute basis. I hit libraries, hit bookstores, and hit health food stores. And then I'd hit the wall.

One night, I had a strange, pivotal experience. Lying on my bed after a long, dreary day of phone calls to the insurance company, I had a sudden, spontaneous vision. I saw my own brain and the upper portion of my spine light up before my eyes, pulsating and glowing bright white, as if I could see *inside* myself. A feeling of nearly superhuman clarity came over me, and I sat up, totally refreshed. I was filled with a vibrant, awakened energy, as if I'd just emerged from a dip in a cold mountain stream. From that instant on, I knew I was going to make it through the strange and frightening ordeal in which I was immersed. I realized that no matter what the outcome, this light that seemed to animate my body would preside over the whole experience, and somehow, I would be fine. I saw that my brain, my mind, and my whole being knew what needed to be done and how to do it, even when *I didn't!*

I'd seen something I could neither grasp nor deny. This light, I knew, would always be shining at some level of my inner being. Even under total sedation. I later told my surgeon that I didn't want any disrespectful talk or weird humor made during the five-hour surgery, which would find me with my head partly separated from my body. And neither did I want any a.m. radio music blaring! He assured me that only Vivaldi was played in his operating rooms, and we shook on the deal. His handshake was firm and strong, and he looked me straight in the eye when he spoke. I saw that he was taking me in on many different levels, and I knew that, to the extent I could trust anyone to make a foot-long incision into my neck, I could trust him. I knew it.

When you stop to think about it, *The Wizard of*

Oz is a very magical and far-out tale. Our brains are like that. Capable of great imagination and creativity, they can manufacture horrible, dreadful demons to terrify us, and they can also work to calm and soothe us, to bring balance back into our beings. In today's precarious, over stimulating world, we're forced to make decisions all day long regarding what we allow to cross the screens of our minds. For most of us, there's a need to be highly selective about our intake.

It's hard for the driven minds of today to relinquish their hold on knowledge and facts and to trust the native wisdom we have within ourselves—our inspiration; our deeper, instinctive knowing; our own biological drive to survive. My uncle was a brilliant man, though he had no more than a high school education. Why? Because he followed his own rhythm and trusted his natural abilities. He knew who he was and had faith in his vision. He listened and spoke from his own spirit and invited us to dance along with him. He cultivated his brain with exercise and good food, with good art and interesting thoughts, and with joyful friendships. Then he trusted those comical feet and his long, rubber legs to take him where they, and he, most wanted to go.

Along with Gene, his piano player, Uncle Ray rehearsed in his backyard studio for hours every day until he was in his seventies and had to have his hip replaced. He was always in great physical shape and ready. Ready for anything. He kept his body fit and limber, giving him extraordinary energy to push into new realms of creative movement and thought. He was excited about what might lie around the next corner. For in life, as in Oz, something unexpected always lies around the next corner. Our brains never grow tired of learning and exploring. Rather, they thrive on it! They thrive on generating new pathways of insight, brand new combinations of ideas, and ever expanding views of the possibilities around us.

The brain has so many amazing powers: the power to heal; the power to guide, to dream, to remember, and to solve problems; the power to see clearly and broadly, to formulate new insights. You name it, and your amazing brain does it. Why not use it wisely and sensitively to revitalize ourselves, to create visions of health and hope to nourish our souls and our planet? Let's expand our understanding of the connections between ourselves and all living things and send our light and wisdom to coming generations. We can't afford to underestimate ourselves now. We are capable of this synthesis. We are made for this discovery.

Since his death in 1987, I've had many dreams of my uncle Ray. In each and every one, he is a young man of twenty-five or so, a man in his prime. He is dressed to perfection, and he is always dancing—making up exquisitely funny, intricate moves; enjoying himself thoroughly; and encouraging me to do the same—to let go and have fun. Why, just last week he appeared in a dream telling me not to procrastinate on writing this story. It would be just like Uncle Ray to try to dance his way back into life, and if anyone could find a way to travel through space and time to get his message across to us, he might just be the one.

Isn't it time to listen to the wisdom of the Scarecrow, to learn to use our powerful brains as carefully and humanely as possible? It's not just a pleasant pastime to confer with flowers and consult with the rain. It's critical to our survival. The balanced brain, in touch with Mother Earth and the plight of our own fellow human beings, is the only sane frontier left to pursue.

SHARING OUR GIFTS

I can see myself now sitting in yet another cramped, stuffy hospital waiting room. Fatigue and worry hang heavy in the air. We all sit quietly with our magazines, reading about various trivial and urgent matters of the day, waiting to see if our blood reports indicate drastically shortened lives.

Not once did I sit in one of these rooms without having the thought that it was totally unnatural for intelligent people to sit and read magazines in a group and never speak to one another—such a waste of time and precious energy when crucial information, support, and comfort could be offered. Yes, even in a room full of "strangers." On more than one occasion I found myself rebelling against the stifling inertia and awkward coldness of these rooms.

Sitting directly across from me in the head-and-neck-surgery waiting room one day was a young

African American woman. This attractive woman of around thirty was trying to stifle the sounds of her weeping as she sat alone, struggling to hold a trachea tube in her neck in place. I saw her and listened to her, and I have to confess that my first reaction was one of stark terror. There was some possibility that the cancer I had could have spread into my trachea, and my initial thought was, "Please, God, don't let that happen to me."

Then I looked around and saw everyone sitting, heads bowed and turning pages while our fellow human being sat in pain-filled isolation, her life altered forever, her sense of herself obviously challenged. When I could stand it no longer, I got up and walked over to her, put my hand on her shoulder, and said the only thing I could think to say, since I was feeling about as lost as she probably was. "I want you to know I care about you," I said. She looked up at me through her tears and tried to tell me something that I couldn't make out, and I added, "Let me know if there is anything I can do for you, okay?"

Within seconds, the woman wiped her tears, got up, and headed for the receptionist's desk, empowered to take an action on her own behalf. It made me feel so good—so much less fearful for my own condition—because if we are here for one another, if we are a family who takes care of one another, then there really isn't so much to be afraid of. What's scary is feeling alienated and alone in our fear and confusion, and this should never be the case. No one in a hospital setting should sit alone in a corner weeping. So much of healing ourselves involves healing our emotions, revealing our tears, and receiving comfort and assurance that we are a deeply valued part of the whole.

Dorothy certainly must have felt like an alien in Oz. We all feel alienated at times. We know that our journeys on earth are temporary, that things can change in the blink of an eye. This is reasonable cause for anxiety. It is also cause for extraordinary compassion for the vulnerable human situation we find ourselves in. Dorothy learned to see herself in her strange new world and say, 'Even here there is love and friendship that I will cherish forever.' All that we can count on to never disappear is the kinship we feel and share with one another. The love we experience. We can make these loving connections in any situation at any time, even in a hospital waiting room. They may be only the briefest of encounters, but they will last a lifetime and perhaps beyond.

People are upset about our medical system today. It's easy to feel alienated there at times. But you needn't see yourself as an alien. Be yourself, honest and truthful about your feelings. Reach out to others. Even the doctor you are seeing may have more pain in his life than you do. In fact, you probably have something to offer him! Remember: People are not the masks or the white coats they wear. We're all human beings who make mistakes and require compassion.

The medical world will improve greatly by realizing the importance of listening to us more deeply and encouraging us with a good word. If we aren't in this together, all of us will lose out. Let's all take this stance and move in the direction of connecting the family of humankind. There's no time left to waste. Life is only worth living if we love one another and do something about it. There's no gesture too small, no single crumb of love or caring offered that can fail to bring some positive result and may bring on a whole series of good results, which we'll never even know of.

In some spiritual traditions, a little string of beads is used to help one keep account of each day's worthy deeds. For each small act of love or sacrifice made, a bead is pushed from one end of the strand to the other. If, at the end of the day, all the beads remain unmoved, it has not really been such a wisely spent day. Surely we can remember to do one small act each day that will benefit another person or the health and well-being of the planet itself—picking up a piece of trash, smiling and speaking to an unknown person, waving someone else into "our" parking space. The reward is great for all of us. Dorothy and her friends got to the Wizard safely for one reason—they linked arms and stuck together.

If Uncle Ray was something of a ham at times, well, perhaps he had a good idea. In any public setting, he was usually visiting and spreading his humor around, generally hamming it up. You had to admit he was having fun and everyone responded enthusiastically. Over the years, I've heard nothing but wonderful things about him from a huge variety of fans and people whose lives he touched personally, as well as those who felt a deep, familial connection to him as the Scarecrow. It's as if he had a sense of mission about his life, to reach people with his own inner experience of love, to shine his light into an otherwise drab situation. Maybe what we need are more Scarecrows to tilt their heads and warm us with their quizzical smiles, more people willing to put aside pride and let their true, loving spirits hang out. That was certainly Uncle Ray's forte—letting it hang out, stuffing and all!

One of my uncle's favorite habits was amusing the tour buses that passed by his house. Hearing the voice of the tour narrator out in front, he jumped up from the lunch table and ran out onto the lawn to do one of his incredible high kicks for the folks from Philadelphia or Omaha. To him, if you felt like running out and doing a high kick in the yard, why not do one? It was only natural. Then he'd return and finish his lunch.

Imagine what this funny surprise encounter with the Scarecrow might have meant to someone on that bus. My uncle did it for just that reason. With life feeling fragile, scary, and challenging to just about everyone these days, it's important we share our talents and uplifting energies broadly. This isn't the time to hold back our gifts or our celebration of life. Offering others what brings you joy or peace will energize everyone. We can't afford to do less than our best. Much is at stake, and every bit of good energy we muster helps hold the world in balance when violence and disturbance surround us.

Each of the characters in *The Wizard of Oz* is called to find his own special virtue or gift. Whether courage, brains, or heart, each wants to grow and make his unique contribution to the whole. Then they join together and support one another in order to complete their journey. One person cannot possibly possess the range of abilities needed to live well in this world. It is through relying on others with some degree of trust, and sharing our individual gifts with others that we become most fully human. When sharing and trust break down, everything breaks down. When human communication lacks support and mutuality, all lose strength and wholeness is impossible. A house divided against itself cannot stand.

Take a moment to remember the wonderful moments you've shared with others. Be grateful for each and every one of them. Can't you easily recall the good feelings they gave you? It's good to dwell on those feelings with joy and gratitude from time to time. Those good feelings and memories are permanently etched on your brain, and you can call them up at any time. Let those good feelings inspire you to connect with life in a new way today. We're created to share our gifts with the whole of life. How could you add some of your light to the world?

Do you have a gift for noticing the needs of others?

Can you make people laugh?

Do you enjoy adding beauty to things?

Do you like to sing or whistle throughout the day?

Do you play a musical instrument?

Do you have a friendly smile?

Are you a peaceful, serene presence?

A good listener?

Are you highly organized or efficient?

Can you fix or build things?

Help with a garden?

Could you offer an apology?

Or make a special meal?

Can you write a card to someone?

Can you pay someone a compliment?

Can you visit a sick friend or call someone in a nursing home?

Speak to a neighbor you've never spoken to?

Could you donate money to a good cause?

Can you practice patience with yourself?

Teach a class at a local library or church?

Can you volunteer for a mentoring program?

Work on your own art form?

Or write a letter to the newspaper?

We each have a part to play in the journey toward wholeness. What is yours? Dust it off. Polish it up. Offer it freely everywhere you go. No gift is too small. And small gifts are usually the best! You'll ignite the spark of life in someone else, and that person will do the same for another. You may not realize the effect of a single act of joyful giving, but like turning on a light in a pitch-dark room, it changes everything. Absolutely everything.

THE NERVE

Looking back in memory now, I find myself on a jungle safari in the big grove of bamboo reeds and azalea plants that lined the length of the Bolger backyard on Beverly Drive. As children, we found this moist thicket a place of great enchantment, of deep darkness and mystery. One traveled into the heart of this mystery at some considerable risk, for the brush was thick and the vines could snare young ankles that trod deeper into the forbidden forest. My older brother took no small delight in seeing that the adventure had its share of terror, assuring me it was, for all intents and purposes, a suicide mission.

Still, there was an overpowering urge to crouch and crawl in and among those green creatures, to take their assaults and emerge on the other side a scraped but victorious traveler. The impulse was to delve in deep for no other reason than to put oneself in a challenging position, to experience the strength of one's character and see if one did or did not have the necessary courage.

Even in the meticulously groomed backyard, we knew we could be lost, held hostage for eternity, or devoured by hungry Bamboolians. Yet, time and again we marched back into the forest of no return, for the alternative, succumbing to fear, was unthinkable. With each passing year, the bamboo forest grew smaller and smaller until I could no longer fathom how we had ever imagined it as we had.

Embarking on a journey from which we may or may not return requires a kind of fortitude and fearless spirit I did not believe I possessed at the outset of my journey into the maze of cancer. The sense of aloneness I experienced can never adequately be described, even to myself, for it was far beyond words. I only knew that in each and every second, I was called on to trust. To trust the light I had seen that, for all my fear and confusion, claimed to know how to navigate the dark jungle of my own terror. I chose to return again and again to believing that this was true. Courage, it seems, is choosing to trust fully in what we cannot see or really know.

One of my most memorable experiences with cancer was an episode that occurred after my first surgery. Awakening from anesthesia, I had the great surprise of finding myself, my conscious awareness, hovering above me on the ceiling of the recovery room! Looking down on the proceedings below, my initial thought was that the recovery room seemed unbelievably primitive. From this unique vantage point, all the latest technology and machinery looked large and clumsy, and the staff seemed to be moving in slow motion. I had the feeling I was viewing the scene from some time in the future or from some other plane of reality. In this unusual moment, I had a clear and certain knowing that what I was looking at was not the medicine of the future. I knew that medicine would one day be simpler, much more refined, and it would not involve in any way the bulky machines I saw nurses and orderlies laboring to drag around the room.

When body and mind were back in synch, I was trapped in misery beyond belief, tangled up in tubes, incapable of calling for help, and violently sick to my stomach for ten hours. Later, I learned that any number of simple solutions could have been added to the anesthesia and prevented the nausea altogether. Live and learn!

None of this is said to criticize contemporary medicine or the many fine people who practice it, but only because I know it is true. There are healing modalities on the horizon which will make the kind of medicine we practice today almost obsolete. These are among many great blessings that await us as we press on with courage in search of more natural methods of healing, based on the understanding that body, mind, and spirit are one and that all illness must be examined from all of these levels. We are not a collection of body parts working independently and mechanically but subtle and mysterious beings who are uniquely and wonderfully made. One day, this will be unchallenged truth, and healers and patients will work together in the spirit of communion and shared insight, which is ultimately our greatest, most powerful healer.

My uncle was years ahead of his time in understanding what physicists now know is the real nature of life, the connectedness of all things. My aunt considered my uncle a creative genius and egged him on in every imaginable way, scrutinizing each of his new dance steps and daring him to outdo himself. Uncle Ray was an original. He worked and played with whatever materials he had at hand rather than waiting for something else to come along. He picked up inanimate objects and interacted with them, talked to them, danced with them. And in seeing these things as important and valuable, he brought them to life in new and delightful ways. He knew that the creative possibilities in any given set of circumstances are virtually limitless. Granted, we often thought he was living in his own little world, but he didn't seem to care. It took courage for him to see life differently and to share his vision with all of us. If we had our doubts now and again, well, that was fine too. He planted his creative seeds and hoped that those seeds would bear good fruit.

We are actually much more aware beings than we realize or give ourselves credit for. With courage we can choose to learn about and access states of being that exceed our often limited views of ourselves. We can always outdo what we think we can do. Something can touch us and open up new worlds of understanding. We can live beyond our present assumptions about ourselves and our lives. There's always more to life than meets the eye. Much, much more indeed.

We're here on earth to learn and to find answers to the deep tangles of life. We must choose, and to choose well, we need courage—courage to face the unknown, to let our guards down long enough to see beyond ourselves, to innovate and invent new possibilities. Courage to try the untried option, which, ironically, is often the most obvious option at hand. The creative capacity of mind is evolving rapidly in our species now. It's up to us to choose whether it will be used for good purposes or for ill. Originality and even perfection are indeed possible when our vision of life is benevolent, open, and just. We are blessed with the freedom to choose such a vision. We only need the courage.

We are living in unknown territory these days. Familiar signposts are few. For many there is a strange sense that we are heading into a forest of no return. The courage we need to face our challenges will come from one place, from our hearts. The word *courage*, after all, comes from the French word *couer*, which means just that: of the heart. We need the strength of heart and the "nerve" of lions to see us through.

GOING HOME

"There's no place like home..." This most-often quoted line from *The Wizard of Oz* gives us something important to think about. Most of us spend our lives in search of an elusive place of comfort and acceptance, a place where safety, love, and warmth permeate the atmosphere. But few people, if the truth is known, feel totally at home in this world, or with themselves, for any great length of time.

As the reality of my diagnosis became clear to me, I saw that my own definition of home was going to have to expand tremendously. I read and prayed and taught myself about a home I could live in forever with or without the body I'd come to regard as myself. I learned how not to look beyond today but to embrace the fullness of each moment as my home and find all the beauty and richness I could within that moment.

The message of Glinda, the good witch of the north, is reliable here. When she tells Dorothy, "The power to get home has been with you all the time," she's talking about a loving, internal home. When we see Glinda's golden light approaching, we're relieved of our fear. Dorothy will be safe. Glinda's light will outshine the darkness. She is wisdom and power personified, and if we give her the time, she'll come to our hearts and allay our fears. She can come from one minute to the next and release us from stress when our egos try to insist that we should have all the answers ourselves. She reminds us to let go, trust, and believe, and what she says will be as true in a thousand years as it was a thousand years ago. When you stop everything and breathe quietly and restfully, when you listen without demand, she appears, warm and reassuring. Everything is going to be all right.

The power to find home lies within us and nowhere else. Without even tapping our heels, we can be home the minute we grant ourselves permission to be. When we stop struggling for ways to change, improve, or escape ourselves, we can be at home right where we are, as we are. Home is within your own heart when it is touched by the soft light of gentle wisdom. This is the peaceful home we are all seeking, a few moments of true sanity, without fear, without worry for the future. For me, going home now means sitting, breathing quietly, and waiting until I remember, once again, that there's no better home than my own heart. If it's not here right now, it's nowhere to be found.

In May of 1997, we had the heart-wrenching task of dismantling Uncle Ray's big home on Beverly Drive. The traditional, white, colonial-style house with green shutters and doors, built in 1915, is one of the few original homes remaining in Beverly Hills. The large pool in the backyard was surrounded by multicolored roses, a large tomato garden, and an expanse of green lawn. My uncle Ray's rehearsal studio sat just beyond the tennis court, amidst avocado and citrus trees that we plucked at year around. (Fortunately, they never retaliated!) My aunt and uncle were contented with their life at home. In their later years, they were private people, delighted to be at home together savoring the quiet, well-ordered life they had spent years creating.

Days after my aunt's funeral, we had the outland-ish, unthinkable task of entering that sacred privacy and, piece by piece, dismantling fifty years of their intimate solitude. It was an uncomfortable assign-ment, going through drawers and closets we had never seen either of them opening. There was a tremendous feeling of violation, of being where one had no busi-ness at all being. Yet the fact remained that this work had to be done and my aunt had requested we do it as quickly as possible. We were invited to take anything we wanted from the house. No stipulations whatsoever were made about things going to certain people—just go through and take what you need.

In her later years, my aunt became completely disinterested in property and things. She took to wearing my uncle Ray's old dress shirts instead of the nice things from her own full closets of designer wear and even spoke of her earlier years of luxury and trav-eling about in style as being baffling to her. She said she often looked back and wondered, "What was *that* all about?" I was amazed at her candor, for those early years had seemed to strongly define her, a woman of impressive sophistication, culture, and intellect. Then it all became irrelevant and she spent her time reflecting on her girlhood in Montana, her first boyfriend from the Indian reservation in Poplar, the little award she'd won at school for playing the piano.

As the end of her life neared, she was piecing things together, sorting out the important from the frivolous. She remembered crocuses peeping out from beneath the snows on the plains. She was detaching from the physical world, living in the realm of emotional memory—not reliving the big events but the singular moments that bore meaning, that helped her make sense of her whole life.

She became a kind of sphinx sitting day in and day out in her blue chair, a horribly uncomfortable thing that she refused to part with. She was exploring the vast region of a mind that had seen many things, spent time with world leaders, made countless hard decisions, seen much tragedy and loss, and learned of itself. She no longer had much interest in the house or her possessions. Like the smart, smart woman she was, she was getting her interior house in order as she prepared to reunite with her husband and her younger brothers gone on before her. She sat in that chair like a woman sitting in a train station reading a magazine. One day, the train pulled in, she put the magazine down, and she got on board. That was it. A quiet, orderly end.

It was odd to see my cousins and siblings wandering through halls and down into basements taping their names onto various things, like supermarket sweepstakes. One of my brothers and his wife tagged furniture and kitchen supplies for their growing household, while another brother spent days in the library alone, meticulously examining each and every book—books of plays, art books, classic literature. I was stricken with a bout of complete disorientation. Without my aunt and uncle to own all these things, they seemed lifeless and unimportant, the mystery and forbidden nature of them stripped away. In the bright light of the afternoon sun, I saw that they were just old pieces of furniture, some well worn and others rather neglected.

Then there was sorting through drawers and closets, each hat and pair of shoes pricking the imagination, my uncle's belongings hanging neatly in his closet, untouched in the many years since his death.

It was hard not to ponder everything deeply, to hold each little item and drift off into a story about where it might have been, what it might have seen—his wristwatch, his wallet full of credit cards, his well-worn tap shoes. Then the admonition that we were to get this job done sooner rather than later, and once again, the scramble to determine what to keep and what to part with forever. At one point of bewilderment, I sat down alone on the staircase and asked if there was anything my aunt would like me to have, and if so, where was it?

At once, my body literally walked me up the stairs and down the hall to her bedroom, directing me to the top of one of several large dressers. There stood a beautiful Italian Madonna carved in oak, with delicately painted doors that opened and shut. I held the sacred item in my hands, amazed. My aunt had never demonstrated a religious nature, not one word or allusion to it in all the years I'd known her. That was Uncle Ray's department, it seemed. Nonetheless, I couldn't help feeling that she had led me to find this special treasure, and indeed, it is the thing I most value of all that she has given me.

Did she really guide me to it? I don't know. But I had never laid eyes on it in my life, nor had I ever heard my aunt speak about her beliefs or her faith. I carry this Madonna with me wherever I go. It keeps me mindful of the fact that somehow, inexplicably, we are always guided to the things that are of true and lasting value to us. And in the end, these very special things, places, people, and moments are all part of what we come to know as home. The place where love and peace live in our hearts.

Not long ago, I drove down Beverly Drive to see how the dear old house was holding up. Pulling up to the curb, I was surprised to see the front door ajar. After a time of wondering about it, I couldn't resist going to the porch to see if I might peek in. I was greeted by a nice Iranian woman who introduced herself as Farah. I felt a strong connection with her and was struck by the intensity of her dancing eyes. She welcomed me in and led me through the house room by room. We chatted about what used to be where and what she had done to make the house home for her family. Rounding each corner, I expected to see Uncle Ray pop out in his flannel shirt and baseball cap. Looking into my aunt's room, I couldn't hold back my tears.

"Are you crying?" Farah asked me.

"A little," I said, swallowing hard and holding a hand to my heart.

"Well, sit down," she said. "Do you like Turkish coffee?"

We sat at the breakfast table where I'd sat for lunch with my aunt and uncle for so many years. A vase of roses from the backyard sat right on the spot where my aunt always placed them. A warm California breeze floated in through the French doors that led out to the pool where I'd learned to swim as a little girl. Something here seemed utterly unchanged.

Farah's mother was the one who had loved the old house and urged Farah to buy it. She sensed a special harmony in it and moved in with Farah's family to live her final days there. Farah showed me a picture of the old woman, and I nearly gasped. She bore an astounding resemblance to *my* grandmother, who also lived her final years in the house. My grandmother had been a mystic and an ardent student of theosophy, the same philosophy that inspired L. Frank Baum's writings. For a moment, I wondered if the two old women might be upstairs enjoying a pot of tea, sharing their uncommon insights. I had to agree, the house felt incredibly peaceful, alive, and open.

Farah told me she too had once returned to Iran and knocked at the door of her childhood home. Her reaction had been similar to mine. In fact, the more we visited, the clearer it became that despite completely different backgrounds, we had a great deal in common. Farah told me she had friends all over the world, people of every nationality, race, and creed.

"I like all kinds of people," she said. "People I don't even know. I smile at people wherever I go, and they smile at me. It's wonderful!"

"Farah," I said, "my uncle Ray would have loved you."

"The funny thing is," she said, "I was getting ready to leave just before you came. I've been trying to leave the house all morning and haven't been able to get off. Perhaps it was because you were coming by!"

"And I circled the block several times myself," I told her, "before I actually came up to the door."

Our eyes met in deep, silent recognition, and we

smiled the wonderful, knowing smile of the inner-most heart.

"Well, perfect timing it seems!" we agreed.

And it always is when you let your heart's wisest instinct guide you home.

THE FAITH OF
THE FOUR

Who is the Wizard of Oz, I wonder, if not a symbol for an all-seeing, omnipotent God? A source that knows and loves all creation. One who designed all the questions and holds all the answers? The entire story is one about faith. Who is the Wizard? Does he really exist? Will he help us? Is it worthwhile searching for him through all the perils of the journey? And are we worthy to stand toe to toe with him? This is what the story is about and why, I believe, it persists and builds momentum with each passing year.

This is a movie most American children and adults see over and over again throughout their lives, never getting their fill of it. Why? Because, in addition to being a great adventure and a poignant tale full of lovable characters, it is a representation of our own deepest drive to determine once and for all if there is a Wizard we can truly believe in, and if so, where is he and what is our connection with him?

In this story, the Wizard that the foursome thinks they will find is an out-and-out fraud, all spectacle and noise. He cannot fulfill their hopes in the way they expect him to, and they are deeply disappointed and rightfully very angry with him. But the story doesn't end there, with four noble, exhausted seekers left to sort things out on their own. No, they are shown instead how to reframe their questions and perspectives. They're offered an entirely new outlook, guided to better see and understand their own predicaments and find the spirit of truth that already lives within each of them. Suddenly, they are able to become the miracle they were hoping and expecting to be given.

The journey to the Wizard was long, difficult, and frightening, but with each and every step, they acquired experience, depth, trust, and resiliency. They garnered the wisdom to believe the truth about themselves once they heard it. They gratefully accepted their new understanding, and then they set off to live it!

Are we, today, willing to settle for somewhat satisfactory answers in our lives rather than following the Yellow Brick Road to where the final truths lie? Do we have the courage and heart, the inner determination, to keep searching until we are convinced one way or the other if the Wizard does in fact exist? Are we willing to risk everything to find out who we are?

Thinking about Uncle Ray's funeral at the Good Shepherd Church in Beverly Hills takes me to a place in my mind that feels important and difficult to recreate. Some things cannot be translated into words, things that overflow with meaning and emotional memory for us. The images run together and are imprinted on us forever in ways that we will never fully understand.

The pageantry of the huge, well-known Catholic church seemed overwhelming to me, not entirely befitting a gentle, bemused old straw man; but on the other hand, very suitable for a devout Catholic seeker whose lifetime of charitable contributions earned him the honored title of Knight of Malta, one of the proudest achievements of his life. Even on that sad occasion, it was somehow wonderful to see hoofers like Sammy Davis Jr. and legends like Jimmy

Stewart filling up the pews to pay their respects to another great one gone on before them. There was a bewildering blend of show business grandiosity and deep eternal spirituality, a strange balance of history and impermanence. I wondered about the many passings that some of these show business giants had witnessed in their incredible lives.

My aunt was the portrait of dignity and restraint. There was never any doubt that she would be. Every morning for the past year, one of us had driven her to Culver City to the small Catholic nursing home where my uncle spent his final days gazing silently out the window at St. Francis, who was overseeing life in the small, flowered courtyard.

I am grateful my aunt hadn't listened to the advice I offered her several days earlier. On that particular day, she felt weak and was very short of breath and considering not making the trip across town. I told her I thought it would be acceptable, under the circumstances, to take the day off and rest. I was sure Uncle Ray would be fine. Hearing that from me somehow made her realize it was, in fact, completely unacceptable to take a day off. She quickly pulled on her trademark red sweater with the gold buttons, put on her lipstick, grabbed a purse, and went directly to the home where my uncle Ray died peacefully in her loving arms within the hour.

A month later, she was rushed to UCLA Medical Center at midnight for emergency coronary bypass surgery, a challenging procedure that she took entirely in her stride. Until the time of her own death, ten years later, she frequently retold the story of her greatest accomplishment with typical, well-earned pride.

"I never missed a single day of visiting your uncle Ray!" she often reminded me. It occurs to me now that I never heard him, even once, referred to as anything other than *"your uncle Ray."* It was as though she wanted, always, to underscore the relevance of his place in our lives and the role she had played in his life providing him with a large, lively family to love him.

I am lost in these and a thousand other reminiscences when a single voice of rare clarity and strength cuts like a bolt of lightning across the huge sanctuary. I reel around to see a stately soprano calling out to all of us "a cappella" from the high balcony at the rear of the church:

"Dance, then, wherever you may be. I am the Lord of the dance, said he."

In one haunting, beautiful instant, all the paradoxes of the present situation fall away. The music and the lyrics of this inspired hymn run a golden strand of truth through all of us, linking the present and the parted in a dream of living sound. It is all the timeless dance and we the unwitting dancers. And she soared on:

"You cut me down, and I leap up high. I am the Lord who will never ever die. I live in you, and you live in me. I am the Lord of the dance, said he."

The inevitability of our being, the perfection of the unknowable plan was undeniably felt. It was all so much to hold on to. When the solo ended, there was a long moment of stillness before the organist caused my world to gently and softly cave in around me.

"Somewhere over the rainbow, way up high, there's a land that I've heard of..."

Aunt Gwen was placed beside her lifetime sweetheart ten years later, on May 13, 1997. Monsignor Healy told the story of their incredible love and devotion to ten of us at the most intimate, down-to-earth funeral I have ever had the honor of attending. My brother brought a cassette player and played Uncle Ray singing "Once Upon a Time," a beautiful love song from a show he starred in called *All American.* We all sobbed and then laughed and prayed and said good-bye to the towering little blonde who had worked her magic on all of us from the very beginning. Our lives without our beloved Scarecrow and his muse would never be the same.

THE RETURN

Yesterday I left a vial of my blood at UCLA for my six-month calcitonin-level check. For the coming week, I will live in a state of suspended reality, waiting for my doctor to e-mail me the numbers that have come to mean the difference between life and death. I recall having these same feelings of disbelief and detachment at the time of my diagnosis, the sensation that I am living somewhere between this world and the next one, sitting on a low-lying cloud watching life and people bustling below me. Everything looks so beautiful and precious, yet I can see that for the most part no one comprehends the miraculous, important nature of it all.

I want to penetrate the illusion and knock down every wall that separates people and reach way beyond myself for every morsel of feeling and meaning and connection I can grasp. I want to see everyone deeply, to exclude no one, to smile at everyone, and to share whatever I can share in each and every moment. I want to "be with the people," as my uncle taught me, to be one with all of them on our mysterious, shared journey.

This week, I have the privilege of remembering who I am and what I am here for. I will honor all that I see and appreciate every chance encounter I have. This week, I will feel strangely close to my departed loved ones. Uncle Ray's spirit will leap and laugh within me, and I will hear the strong, wise words of my aunt Gwen guiding me. The songs of the birds will ring in my ears, and the orange poppies in the field across from my house will blaze more brightly. People will look intriguing and open and somehow familiar to me. I will feel like the Wizard and the dazzled Dorothy and all of her companions rolled into one. And I will know, beyond any shadow of a doubt, that all of us are here searching for one and the very same thing, "Love, love, love."

This week, I will truly be alive.

"My life is loving people. It's a difficult kind of world to live in, but it's a great world, because I get satisfaction and I don't have any hang-ups about it! I belong to the people. As long as I can send them home saying, 'Gee, he made me feel happy,' well, that's my life! That's what I work for, to give people joy."

—Ray Bolger

Lightning Source UK Ltd.
Milton Keynes UK
UKHW012147130223
416920UK00002B/486